TOOLS TO PREDICT WEATHER

AN INTRODUCTION TO WEATHER PATTERNS

Earth and Space Science Grade 1

Children's Books on Science, Nature & How It Works

BABY PROFESSOR
EDUCATION KIDS

First Edition, 2024

Published in the United States by Speedy Publishing LLC, 40 E Main Street, Newark, Delaware 19711 USA.

© 2024 Baby Professor Books, an imprint of Speedy Publishing LLC

Baby Professor Books are available at special discounts when purchased in bulk for industrial and sales-promotional use. For details contact our Special Sales Team at Speedy Publishing LLC, 40 E Main Street, Newark, Delaware 19711 USA. Telephone (888) 248-4521 Fax: (210) 519-4043.

10 9 8 7 6 * 5 4 3 2 1

Print Edition: 9781541987265
Digital Edition: 9781541987654
Hardcover Edition: 9781541989023

See the world in pictures. Build your knowledge in style.
www.speedypublishing.com

TABLE OF CONTENTS

Weather is an important part of our lives and it affects what we do.

Have you ever heard someone say, "weather permitting"? It means that they have plans, but they will have to change them if the weather is bad. Have you ever had to cancel your plans because it started to rain? Weather is an important part of our lives. Whether it is hot or cold, raining or sunny, weather affects what we do. Since weather is so important, it is good to know what causes it. Some people have jobs predicting weather. This book will teach you all about why weather is important, what causes it, and how to predict it.

CHAPTER ONE: HOW WEATHER AFFECTS LIFE

Weather is what the _atmosphere_ is like during a certain time in a certain place. The atmosphere goes through changes. These can result in clouds, rain, sunshine, wind, high temperatures or cold temperatures and more.

Weather is what the atmosphere is like during a certain time in a certain place.

It would not be a good idea to wear shorts and a T-shirt outside during winter.

HOW WE DRESS:

How we dress is affected by the weather. It would not be a good idea to wear shorts and a T-shirt when it is snowing. People can die from becoming too cold.

It is also a bad idea to wear a heavy coat, scarves, boots, and mittens on a hot, summer day. People can pass out from the heat.

It is a bad idea to wear a heavy coat, scarves, boots, and mittens on a hot, summer day.

People need different kinds of clothes for different seasons.

The human body makes its own body heat. Our bodies need to be kept at a steady temperature. If we get too hot or cold, it is bad. This is why we need different kinds of clothes.

THE PLACES WE LIVE IN:

The places we choose to live in are also affected by weather. In the desert, for instance, people might have flat roofs. In a rainy or snowy climate, people are more likely to have sloped roofs. That way the rain or snow can fall down the side. If too much rain or snow is stuck on a flat roof, it could cause problems.

In the desert, people might have flat roofs.

In a rainy or snowy climate, people are more likely to have sloped roofs.

In hot climates, people often have air conditioning.

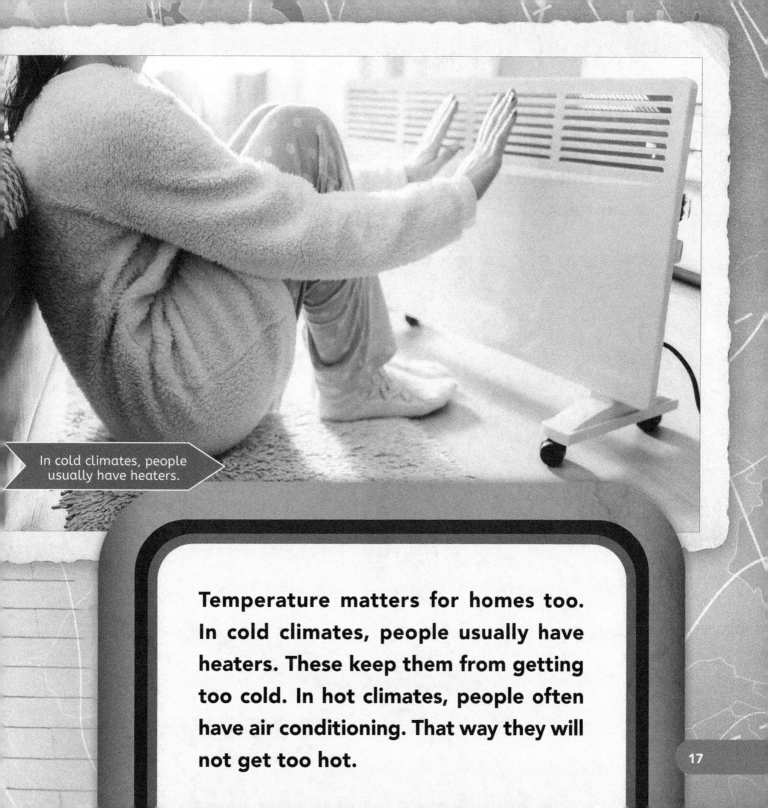

In cold climates, people usually have heaters.

Temperature matters for homes too. In cold climates, people usually have heaters. These keep them from getting too cold. In hot climates, people often have air conditioning. That way they will not get too hot.

WHAT WE DO FOR FUN:

Even what we do for fun is affected by weather. People do not go snowboarding or skiing in deserts. That is something done in places where there are snowy mountains.

People go skiing in snowy mountains.

People who go swimming or surfing usually do it during the summer.

People who go swimming or surfing usually do that during the summer. They also might do it in places that are hot all year around.

WHY WEATHER FORECASTS MATTER:

Not all weather is easy to handle. We can look outside and feel the temperature. That way we can know what to wear or what to do. Sometimes though, weather can become dangerous. This is called severe weather conditions. Weather can also change quite quickly. This is why warnings become important. Good weather _forecasts_ can even save lives.

WEATHER

WORLD NEWS GLO

MMUNITY CELEBRATES A MONTH OF PEACE AND PROSPERITY · BUSINESS

Hurricanes are rainstorms that form over oceans and can be thousands of miles long and last for days.

Hurricanes are an example of severe weather. Hurricanes are rainstorms that form over oceans. They can be thousands of miles long and last for days. Hurricanes have winds that can go as fast as 180 miles per hour! They can destroy homes and cause a lot of damage.

Blizzards are severe snow storms. They can be so bad you cannot see properly. They are so dangerous because they are so cold. The winds can also make it hard to move. People need to take shelter during blizzards and stay warm. Driving during blizzards can also be much more dangerous.

Driving during blizzards can be much more dangerous.

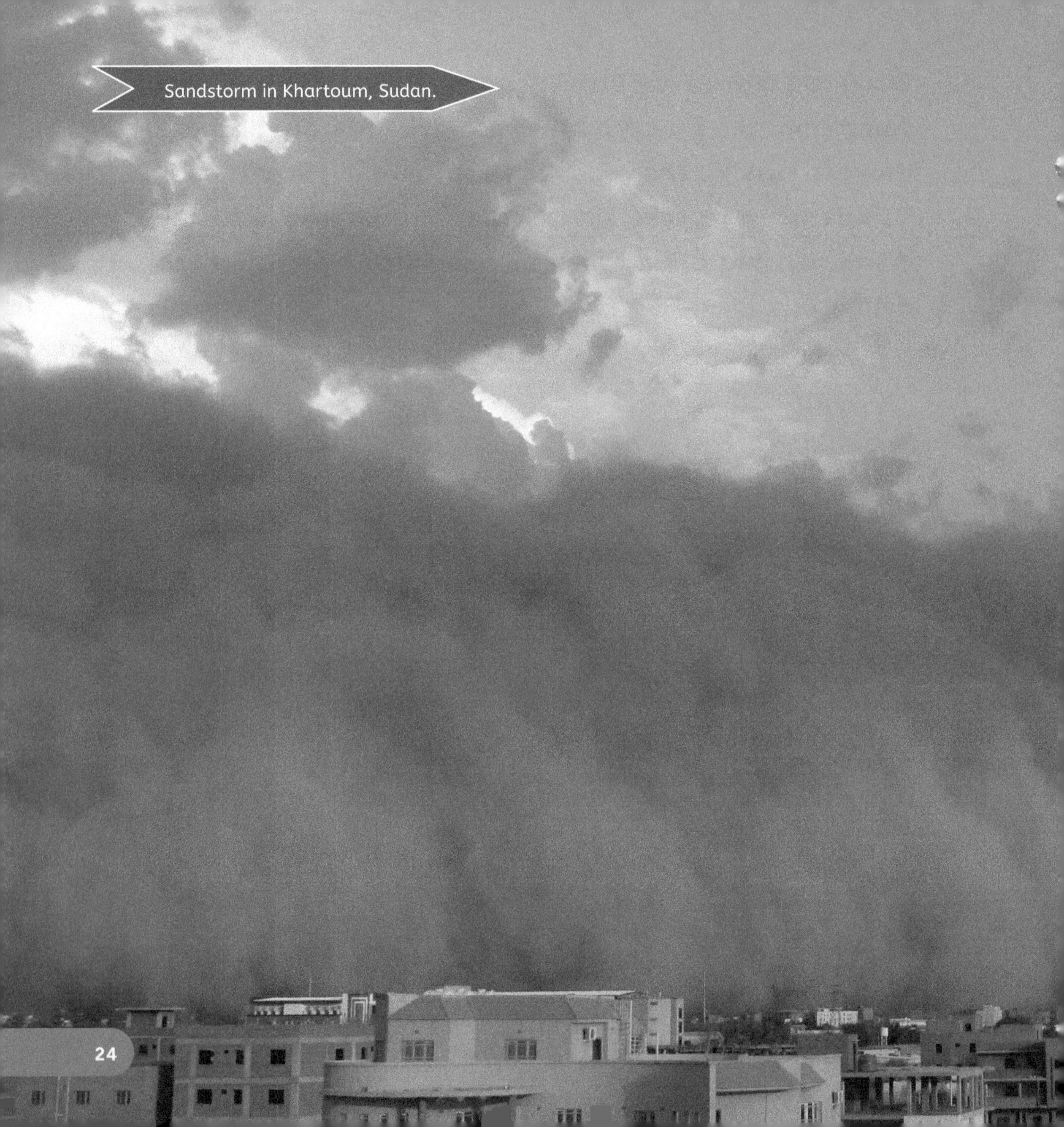

Sandstorm in Khartoum, Sudan.

There are also dust storms in deserts. These are when strong winds pick up dust and sand. They blow it around. These can be dangerous because it is bad for people to breathe the air. Sometimes these dust storms or sand storms are so strong the sand can be like sandpaper! This can cause harm to cars, homes, and even people.

Sometimes if the weather is too hot and dry, there will not be enough rain. This can cause droughts. Droughts are when there is not enough water. This can cause plants to die. Sometimes people will die from lack of water and food too. Other times it can cost people a lot of money. Many farmers rely on rainwater to grow their crops.

Droughts can cause plants to die and sometimes people will die from lack of water and food too.

Too much rain can also be bad. This can lead to mudslides. People can die in mudslides too.

Too much rain can lead to mudslides

Forecasts mean that people will know about these severe weather conditions in advance.

Forecasts mean that people will know about these severe weather conditions in advance. They can stock up on food and water. They will know to stay indoors. They will also be able to leave if it is too unsafe to stay.

CHAPTER TWO:
WHAT CAUSES
WEATHER

Things that affect the atmosphere can affect the weather. This means that how the Sun heats the Earth, the amount of water in the air, and the pressure of the air on Earth all matter.

ATMOSPHERE FACTORS

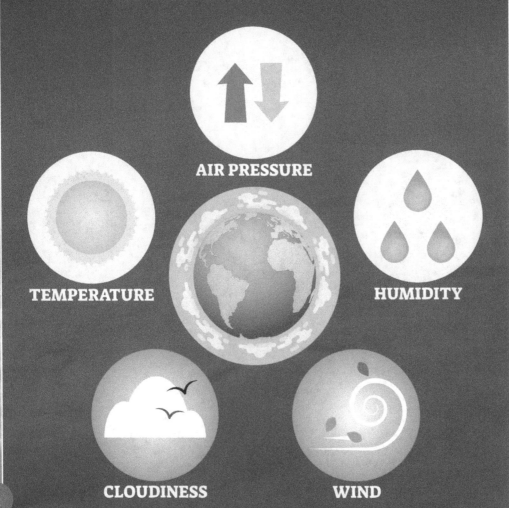

AIR PRESSURE

TEMPERATURE

HUMIDITY

CLOUDINESS

WIND

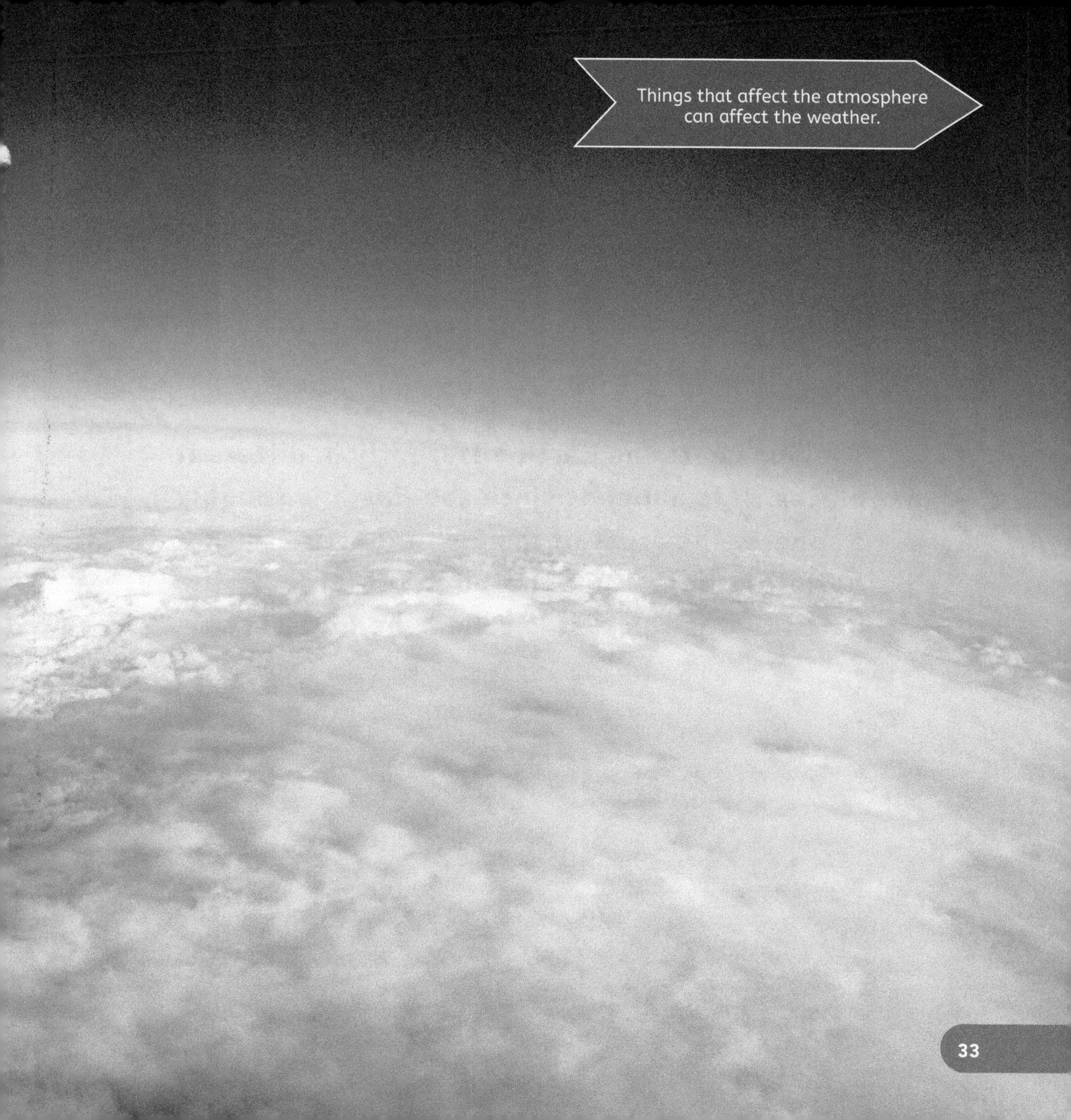

Things that affect the atmosphere can affect the weather.

HEATING THE EARTH:

The Sun heats the Earth differently in different places. This happens since the Earth is roughly a sphere. The areas of the Earth that are thicker get more heat from the Sun. The area of the Earth that is thickest is called the Equator.

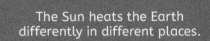

The Sun heats the Earth differently in different places.

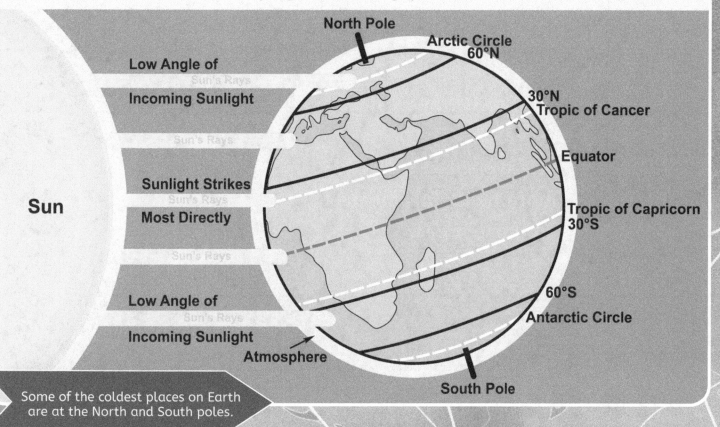

Earth's Vital Areas
(Angle of Sun Rays)

North Pole

Arctic Circle
60°N

Low Angle of Sun's Rays

Incoming Sunlight

30°N
Tropic of Cancer

Sun's Rays

Equator

Sunlight Strikes

Sun's Rays

Most Directly

Sun

Tropic of Capricorn
30°S

Sun's Rays

Low Angle of Sun's Rays

60°S

Antarctic Circle

Incoming Sunlight

Atmosphere

South Pole

Some of the coldest places on Earth are at the North and South poles.

Some of the coldest places on Earth are at the North and South poles. These are some of places that are farthest away from the Sun.

The Earth is also slanted as it goes around the Sun. This is why we have changes in the seasons. The parts of the Earth that are slanted towards the Sun get more heat. This means it is summer in those areas.

NORTHERN HEMISPHER

—EQUATOR

SOUTHERN HEMISPHER

WINTER

SPRING

When the Earth moves to the other side of the Sun, those places are now further away. The season changes to winter in those areas. Meanwhile, the opposite side of the Earth now has summer.

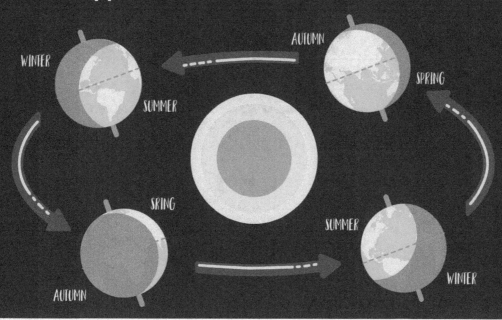

SUMMER   AUTUMN

Have you ever heard that during Christmas in Australia people go to the beach? That is because they are on a part of the Earth that is close to the Sun when it is Christmas. They have summer when people in the United States have winter!

People go to the beach during Christmas in Australia.

The Water Cycle

Condensation

Evaporation

Precipitation

Collection

The water cycle explains how we get precipitation.

THE WATER CYCLE:

The water cycle explains how we get _**precipitation**_. The water cycle begins when water on the ground is heated by the Sun. This causes the water to evaporate. Evaporate means the water becomes gas and goes into the air.

When the water is in the air, it eventually condenses. This means the water turns back into liquid. This is how we get clouds.

The water turns back into liquid which is how we get clouds.

When clouds get heavy enough, the water falls to the Earth. This is how we get rain or snow. It changes based upon how cold it is. Sometimes we can also get _hail_.

When clouds get heavy enough, the water falls to the Earth as rain, snow, or hail.

1000

The water that falls to the ground collects and becomes puddles, and rivers.

The water that falls to the ground collects. It becomes puddles, and rivers. Finally, water ends up in the oceans. This begins the cycle once more.

Some winds are so strong they can become dangerous.

PARTS OF WEATHER:

Apart from precipitation there are other things that affect the weather. One part of the weather is wind. Winds can be gentle or strong. Some winds are so strong they can become dangerous.

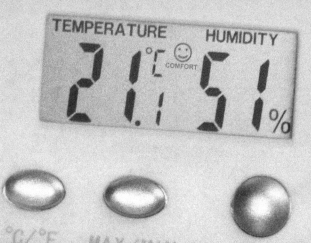

Humidity is another part of weather. It is how much water is in the air. Warm air can carry more water than cold air.

Temperature is another important part of weather. How hot or cold it is affects humidity, wind, and precipitation.

Another part of weather is atmospheric pressure. This is how much the air presses down onto a certain spot. Even air has weight. In large spaces, air can be quite heavy.

These parts all interact to create weather patterns we can predict.

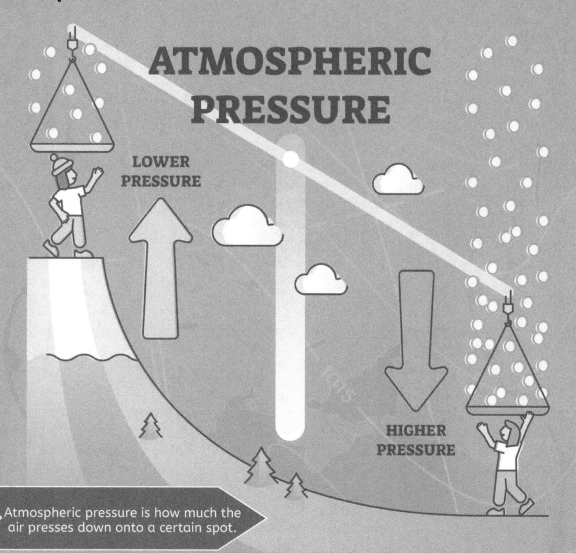

ATMOSPHERIC PRESSURE

LOWER PRESSURE

HIGHER PRESSURE

Atmospheric pressure is how much the air presses down onto a certain spot.

CHAPTER THREE: PREDICTING WEATHER

A meteorologist reading meteodata instruments in modern meteorologic observation station.

Meteorologists are people who study weather. They study and measure the different parts of the weather. They can help make predictions.

Seasons are an example of weather patterns.

WEATHER PATTERNS:

A weather pattern is when the weather stays the same over a period of time. Seasons are an example of weather patterns. Every year, the temperatures get colder during winter months. They get warmer during summer months.

Weather patterns make predictions easier. This is one reason why keeping good _records_ can be important. Rainy weather usually happens in the spring and summer. It is also usually hotter in the summer. It is usually colder in winter.

Another weather pattern is that it is usually colder in the morning than the afternoon. This is because the Sun has had more time to heat the Earth later in the day.

Another weather pattern is that it is usually colder in the morning than the afternoon.

Meteorologists can use these *observations*. They can infer what might happen. An inference is a guess someone makes based upon *data*, observations, and experiences.

Meteorologists can use the observations and can infer what might happen.

CLOUD TYPES:

Different clouds types are also a part of weather patterns. They can be used to infer the weather. Cirrus clouds are clouds that are very wispy and thin. They usually mean good weather. Stratus clouds are gray clouds. They tend to cover the whole sky. If they come down to the ground, they become fog. Cumulus clouds are white, puffy clouds. They can be seen on nice days. Cumulus clouds can grow large and dark. Then they become cumulonimbus clouds. These are the clouds that come with thunderstorms.

Cirrus clouds are clouds that are very wispy and thin.

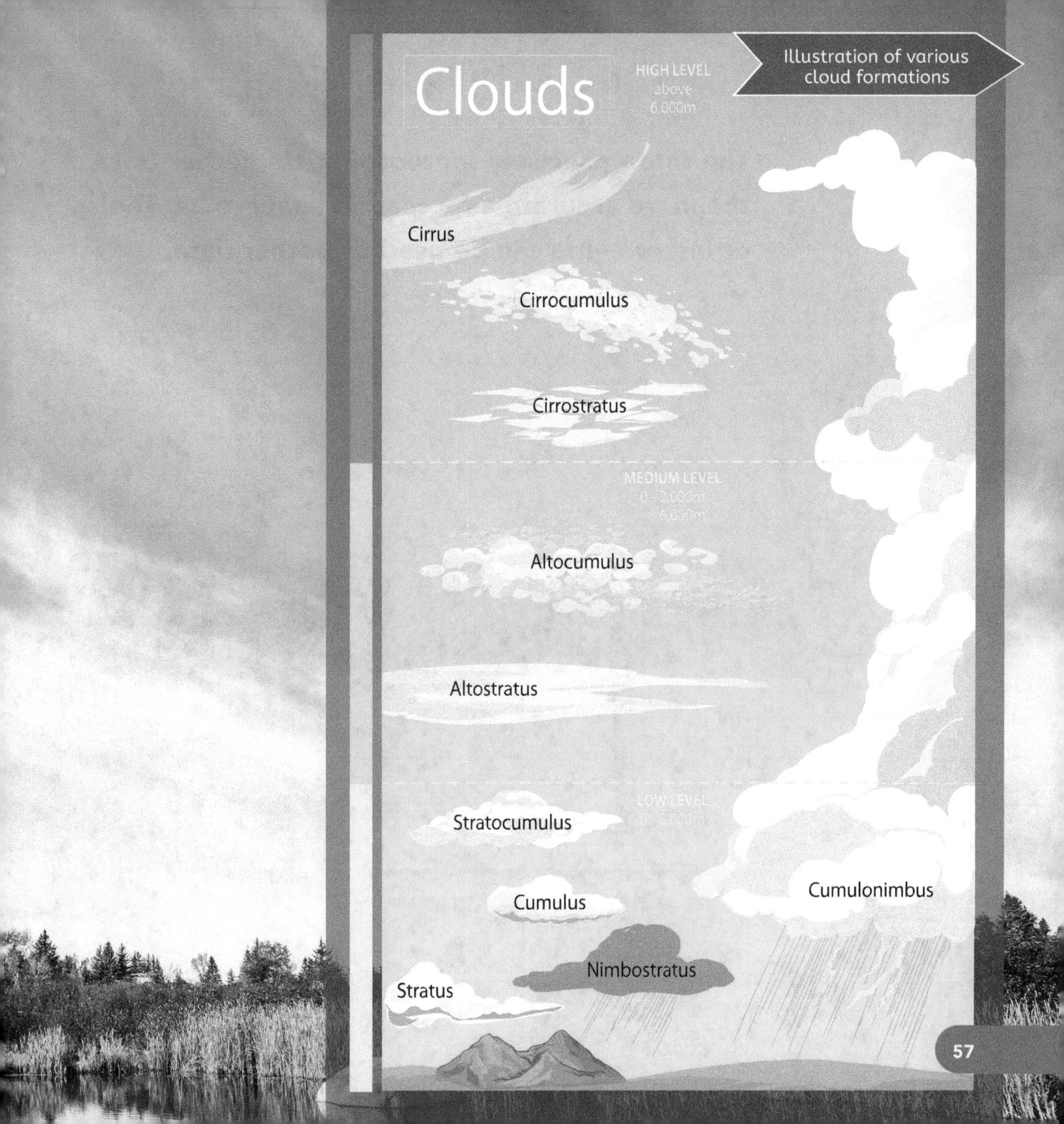

Clouds

HIGH LEVEL
above
6,000m

Cirrus

Cirrocumulus

Cirrostratus

MEDIUM LEVEL
0 - 2,000m
6,000m

Altocumulus

Altostratus

LOW LEVEL
0 - 2,000m

Stratocumulus

Cumulus

Cumulonimbus

Nimbostratus

Stratus

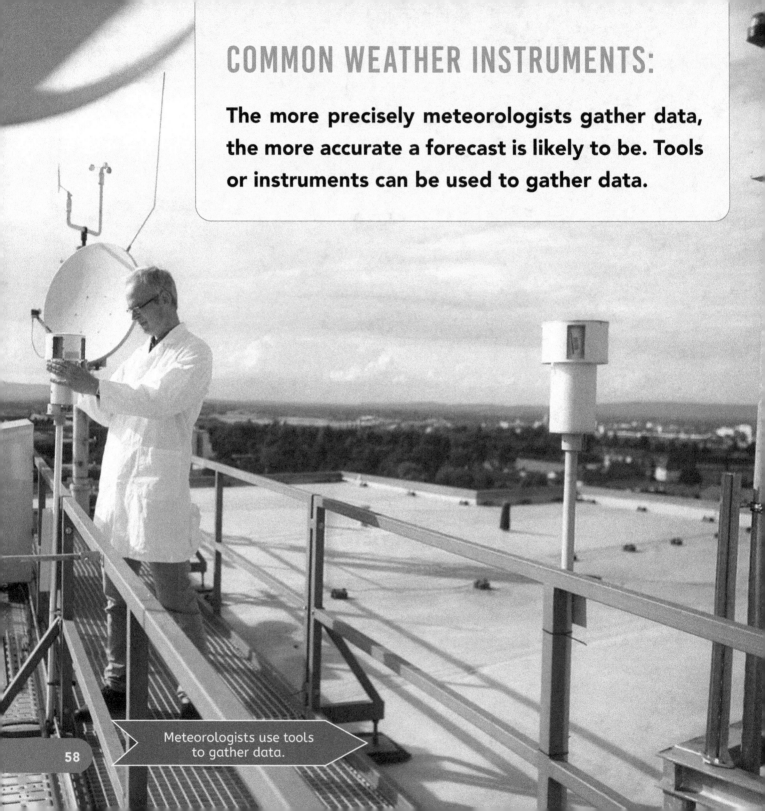

COMMON WEATHER INSTRUMENTS:

The more precisely meteorologists gather data, the more accurate a forecast is likely to be. Tools or instruments can be used to gather data.

Meteorologists use tools to gather data.

A rain gauge is used to measure how much rainfall there is.

Rain gauges are used to measure how much rainfall there is. They are sort of like measuring cups. They are placed outside. The rainwater collects in it. How much it collects is how much rain fell in that area during that time.

°C °F

50   120
40
30   100
20   80
10   60
0   40
10   20
20   0
30   20

Thermometers are used to measure temperature. A lot of thermometers use mercury. The mercury is a liquid that is placed in a tube. The hotter it gets, he higher the mercury goes. This happens because liquids expand when they get hotter.

Barometers measure atmospheric pressure. Often when the atmospheric pressure goes down, it means a storm is coming. If the atmospheric pressure goes up, it means good weather is on the way.

A barometer measures atmospheric pressure.

A wind vane is used to tell wind direction.

Wind vanes are used to tell wind direction. As the wind blows, it hits the vane. The movement of the wind forces the vane around to point in the right direction. If the wind changes direction, the wind vane will move with it.

Weather satellites can take pictures of weather patterns from above the Earth.

WEATHER SATELLITES:

Today computers and satellites help with weather forecasts. Satellites are in Space. This means they can take pictures of weather patterns from above the Earth! These pictures can help meteorologists track weather patterns anywhere in the world.

Computers are also helpful. They can store a lot of data. They can also put years of data into graphs quickly. Imagine having many years of weather data for the month of July. You would be a lot more likely to find patterns.

Computers can store a lot of data and can put years of data into graphs quickly.

SUMMARY

Weather is what we call changes in the atmosphere. It can be how hot or cold, rainy or sunny, windy or still it is outside. Weather patterns affect our lives from how we dress, what we wear, and the houses we live in. Weather can also become severe. Severe weather can be dangerous.

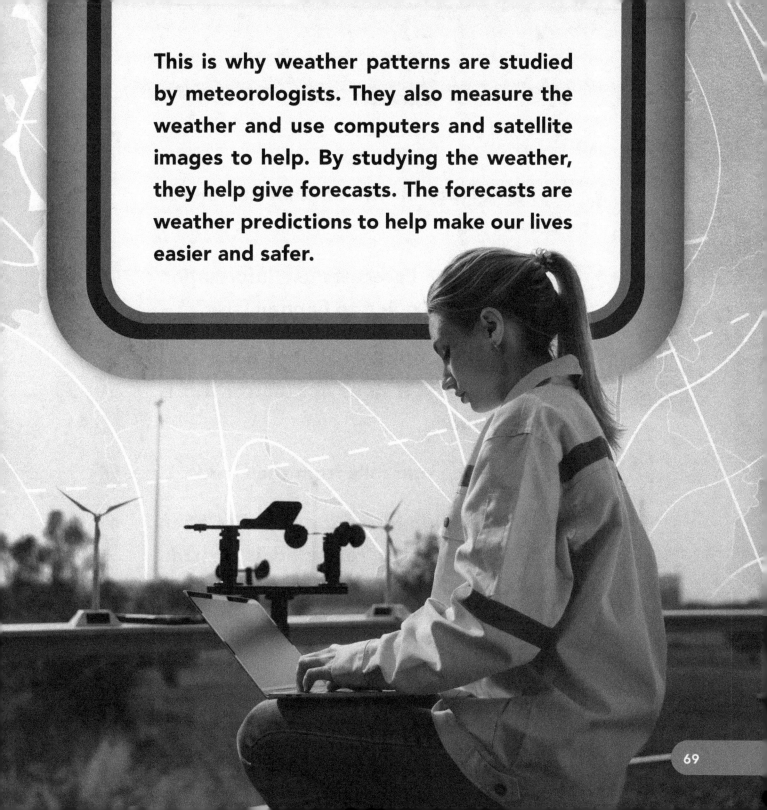

This is why weather patterns are studied by meteorologists. They also measure the weather and use computers and satellite images to help. By studying the weather, they help give forecasts. The forecasts are weather predictions to help make our lives easier and safer.

GLOSSARY

Atmosphere (pg. 8): the air that surrounds the Earth

Forecast (pg. 20): Forecasts use information to predict what is going to happen later.

Precipitation (pg. 40): Any kind of water that falls from the sky. It does not matter if it is frozen or liquid.

Hail (pg. 42): ice that falls from the clouds

Records (pg. 53): information that has been recorded. Something recorded is written down or filmed, so it can be looked at later.

Observations (pg. 55): things we can detect with our senses or our tools

Data (pg. 55): information we collect when we measure things or notice things

Visit

www.speedypublishing.com

To view and download free content on your
favorite subject and browse our catalog of new
and exciting books for readers of all ages.

Printed in the USA
CPSIA information can be obtained
at www.ICGtesting.com
CBHW081443120624
9942CB00060B/435